NEW BOOKS FOR NEW READERS

Phyllis MacAdam, *General Editor*

Three Kentucky Tragedies

Richard Taylor

WITHDRAWN

THE UNIVERSITY PRESS OF KENTUCKY

Cover illustration: From a mural by Ezra Winter at the Clark
National Memorial in Vincennes, Indiana. *Courtesy of the
George Rogers Clark National Historical Park.*

Copyright © 1991 by the University Press of Kentucky

Scholarly publisher for the Commonwealth,
serving Bellarmine College, Berea College, Centre
College of Kentucky, Eastern Kentucky University,
The Filson Club, Georgetown College, Kentucky
Historical Society, Kentucky State University,
Morehead State University, Murray State University,
Northern Kentucky University, Transylvania University,
University of Kentucky, University of Louisville,
and Western Kentucky University.

Editorial and Sales Offices: Lexington, Kentucky 40508-4008

Library of Congress Cataloging-in-Publication Data

Taylor, Richard, 1941-
 Three Kentucky tragedies / Richard Taylor.

   p. cm. — (New books for new readers)
   ISBN 0-8131-0907-8 (acid-free)
   1. Readers for new literates. 2. Readers—Kentucky. 3. Kentucky
—History. I. Title. II. Series.
PE1126.A4T39   1991
428.6—dc20   91-29438

Contents

Foreword

The New Books for New Readers project was made possible through funding from the National Endowment for the Humanities, the Kentucky Humanities Council, the Scripps-Howard Foundation through *The Kentucky Post,* and Financial Women International. The co-sponsorship and continuing assistance of the Kentucky Department for Libraries and Archives and the Kentucky Literacy Commission have been essential to our undertaking. We are also grateful for the advice and support provided to us by the University Press of Kentucky. All these agencies share our commitment to the important role that reading books should play in the lives of the people of our state, and their belief in this project has made it possible.

The Kentucky Humanities Council sees the campaign for adult literacy as closely linked to our own mission, to make the rich heritage of the humanities accessible to all Kentuckians. Because the printed word is a vital source of this heritage, we believe that books about our state's history and culture written for adult literacy students can help us bring the humanities to Kentucky citizens who might not otherwise have the opportunities to participate in our programs. We offer these books in the hope that, in content and by example, they will be of value to adult new readers.

Virginia G. Smith, Executive Director
Kentucky Humanities Council

Preface

The three stories that follow are based on the early years of Kentucky's rich and colorful history. Each is a tragedy in one or more senses. Tragedy, in a literary sense, is about a downfall that results from human failing. The failing may be some flaw in character or the breaking of a moral law. Fate may add to a fall. Because the tragedies of others are about human failing, these tragedies are, in a sense, our own. Tragedy may also be seen in a broader sense as disaster, some unhappy event that causes dread or fear.

As these stories show, the meanings of tragedy are often combined. The first is a tale of love and revenge with a twist. The second is about the fall of a family and the brutal murder of a slave. The last tells of a disastrous battle between Indians and settlers at the end of the American Revolution. In each I tried to follow the historical facts as they are known, but I have added conversation and details in order to be true to the spirit of the events. It has been said that, when telling a story, you should "never let the facts get in the way of the truth."

About the Author: Richard Taylor is the author of one novel, *Girty,* two books of poems, *Bluegrass* and *Earth Bones,* and a forthcoming book on Sue Mundy, a Confederate guerrilla active in Kentucky during the Civil War. Taylor teaches English at Kentucky State University and lives with his wife and three children outside of Frankfort, where he owns Poor Richard's Books.

Acknowledgments

This book has been produced with help from many people. Special thanks are due Lillian Nunnelly, director of adult learning in Franklin County, and the new adult readers and their tutors at the Thorn Hill Learning Center, whose insights and enthusiasm made each reading session a learning experience for all of us: J.R. Ross, Antoinette Herzel, Mary Heilman, Chris Brown, Charles "Chuck" Miller, Lois Jean True, Harold Purvis, James Warren, Ann Carter, and Becky Van Leuven.

Thanks are also due to Phyllis MacAdam, whose support and good advice during every phase of the project were invaluable. Additional thanks to Boynton Merrill, Jr., whose *Jefferson's Nephews,* one of the finest pieces of historical writing about Kentucky that I know, forms the basis of the Lewis narrative. Finally I want to thank Nancy Brooks and Barbara Sharp at Kentucky State University who generously and patiently helped prepare the finished text.

The Beauchamp-Sharp Tragedy

Jeroboam Beauchamp kissed his wife Ann good-bye, saying he would be home in a few days. He climbed onto his horse and set out for Frankfort to kill Solomon Sharp. The time was early November of 1825. He left the Green River country of Western Kentucky and rode northeast toward the state capital. There he knew he would find Solomon Sharp, the man he must kill. When he came to the main road, he put a red bandanna over his head to hide his face.

Jeroboam and his wife lived on a farm in Simpson County. The trip to Frankfort would take four days. On the way he thought about his promise to his wife. Ann had agreed to marry him only if he would kill Colonel Solomon P. Sharp.

Solomon Sharp was a lawyer and politician. As a young man, he was elected to the Kentucky legislature. Then he served in the U.S. Congress. In 1818 he married Miss Eliza Scott of Frankfort. They bought a home in Bowling Green, Kentucky, and started a family. He opened a law office there. But three years later he ran for a seat in the State Senate. He won the election and moved to Frankfort.

Jeroboam was also a lawyer. Born in 1802, he was the second son of Thomas Beauchamp, a small farmer. He grew up in Simpson County, six miles south of the town of Franklin. He went to local schools and later taught school himself. When he tired of teaching, he moved to nearby Glasgow and studied law. He met Solomon Sharp, who hired him to do some legal work. But Jeroboam did not stay long with the law. Young and restless, he moved back to his father's farm in 1820.

There he met Miss Ann Cook. She had been raised in Virginia with every advantage. She was well educated. She wrote poetry. Unlike many women of her day, she was raised to think for herself. Lively and popular, she went to many parties. Then her family lost its property, and her father died. She and her aging mother moved to Kentucky. They came to live with her brother, who owned a small farm near the Beauchamps.

That same year Solomon Sharp was asked to serve as Attorney General of Kentucky. He had a political enemy named John Waring who wanted to put an end to Sharp's political career. Waring printed a handbill accusing Sharp of having an affair with Ann Cook. He was also accused of being the father of Ann Cook's illegitimate child. The baby had been born dead.

When Jeroboam first tried to meet Ann Cook, she was living quietly on her brother's farm. She refused to see him. As an excuse to be with her, he asked to borrow some books. She let him. They began talking about the books he read. After several visits he won her trust, and they became friends. There was a difference in their ages. When they met, Ann was in her late thirties, and Jeroboam was just twenty years old. After a time they became lovers, and he asked her

2

Colonel
Solomon
Sharp

to marry him. At first she refused. Finally, she said
yes on condition that he right the wrong Sharp had done
her. He promised, and they were married in 1824. He
was 21. She was 38.

For a time they lived happily on the farm. Jeroboam
went back to the law again. He did some legal work for
Solomon Sharp, who had moved to Frankfort. There
did not seem to be any hard feelings between Jeroboam
and Sharp. This was soon to change.

In the fall of 1825 Sharp gave up the post of
Attorney General because he wanted to run for the
legislature. He won the election in a close race.
Before he was approved for office, there was another

handbill, this one printed by Sharp's political friends. It claimed that Sharp could not be the father of Ann Cook's baby because it was a Negro.

When the news came to Jeroboam, he decided he must act. As Ann's husband, he felt he had a duty to protect her. She had been dishonored a second time, and he held Sharp and his friends to blame. After telling Ann how he felt, he asked if she still wanted him to kill Sharp. She did.

So Jeroboam set out for Frankfort, planning to murder Sharp. If anyone asked him why he had the bandanna over his head, he would say he had a headache. Along the way he tried to avoid people as much as he could.

He came to Frankfort on the evening of November 6, 1825. The legislature was to meet the next day. There were many strangers in town, and the hotels were full. He finally found a room in the house of Robert Scott, keeper of the state prison. Jeroboam ate supper and then put up his horse. He told Scott he was going to bed, saying he was tired and not feeling well.

When everyone was asleep, Jeroboam got up. He crept down the stairs and quietly left the house. Keeping out of view, he walked several blocks past the capitol building. He stopped before a large brick house on Madison Street, where he knew Sharp lived. The house was two and a half stories high. Living with the Sharps was Dr. Leander Sharp, Colonel Sharp's brother. Jeroboam knew that Colonel Sharp and his wife had their bedroom on the first floor. He also knew the house had a door opening onto the alley. The alley was dark and ran along the side of the house.

Jeroboam waited outside until he was sure all were asleep. About 1:30 A.M. the night patrol passed him on the street. He was sure he had been seen, but no one stopped him to ask questions. The patrol went on. About two o'clock all the lights were out in the house. Jeroboam knew this was the time to act. He crept up to the house and knocked on the side door. When no one came, he knocked again. This time Sharp came to the door. Before opening it, he asked who was there.

"Your friend, John A. Covington," said Jeroboam.

Sharp asked him to repeat his name.

"John A. Covington."

"I know no one by that name," said Sharp. "Why have you come here so late?"

Jeroboam said that he had gotten lost and that all the hotels were full. He asked if Colonel Sharp could put him up for the night.

Sharp stepped back and opened the door. He held out his right hand in friendship. Jeroboam did not take it. He stepped in and asked, "Are you Colonel Sharp?"

"Yes," Sharp said, "but I don't know you." Looking more closely, he cried, "Great God, it's him!"

5

At that moment Jeroboam grabbed Sharp's wrist, shouting, "Die, you villain!"

Sharp saw the knife in Jeroboam's hand and tried to take it away. But Jeroboam threw him to the floor, stabbing him in the chest. Mrs. Sharp, standing in the doorway to the bedroom, looked on in horror. When she saw the knife, she ran back through the house screaming for help. She returned to find her husband lying on the floor, his chest covered with blood. He was groaning but did not speak. He died without saying a word. Jeroboam stood outside the window, waiting to see if he was named. Just as Colonel Sharp died, Mrs. Sharp looked up at Jeroboam. For a second their eyes met. Then he jumped from the window and ran away.

The screams of Mrs. Sharp woke up everyone in the house. Dr. Sharp, the Colonel's brother, was out visiting a patient. Someone sent for him. Lights were lit. When the neighbors came, they saw Mrs. Sharp and her three children crying over the body. Several men moved the body into the front room. There they sat down to talk about what should be done. At first light, they went outside to search for clues. Near a rose bush one of them found a bloody bandanna with two holes in it. There were no footprints.

News of the killing spread over the whole state. The legislature had begun on the day of the murder. Colonel Sharp was to have been made Speaker of the House of Representatives. Instead, his death was announced. After the shock came sadness and anger.

Speeches were given in his honor. The lawmakers agreed to wear black bands on their arms. No one could imagine who killed him, but many thought the killing was political.

In the afternoon the leaders of Frankfort met to talk about what should be done. They put up $1,000 as a reward for the capture of the "monster" who killed Colonel Sharp. Governor Desha added $3,000 to the reward. Friends of the Colonel put up $3,000 more. Little was known about the killer. He had called himself John A. Covington. He was said to be tall and wearing dark clothes.

The funeral was one of the largest held in Frankfort. Almost the whole town came to it. The stone over the grave reads:

To Father
Solomon P. Sharp;
was assassinated while extending
the hand of hospitality on the
morning of Nov. 7, 1825, in
38 year of his age.

The talk in town was about who the killer might be. Some said it was John Waring, who once said he would kill Sharp. But Waring had been shot through the hips the week before. Nor was he near Frankfort at the time of the killing. Then someone brought up the name of Jeroboam Beauchamp. Slowly the pieces were put in place. Someone remembered he had married Ann

Cook. The story about the seduction came up. There were rumors that Beauchamp had said he would kill Sharp. Beauchamp quickly became the chief suspect.

On the morning after the killing someone saw Beauchamp riding south out of town. To catch him, a search party was formed. That evening just at dark, four riders set out for Simpson County, a distance of 165 miles. They wanted Beauchamp back in Frankfort to answer some questions.

Jeroboam had left Frankfort at dawn on the morning after the killing. He stopped for breakfast at an inn eight miles out of town. Though he was asked the news, he didn't mention Sharp's death. That night he stayed with some kin at Bloomfield. He rode the next day to Bardstown where he ate and visited more kin. He stayed all day to rest his horse. The next morning he left for Bowling Green where he had breakfast and saw more of his kin. Then he went south through Franklin and was home at sunset.

As he passed through the gate to the farm, he raised a red flag on a stick. He waved it as he rode up to the house, a sign that he had killed Sharp. When Ann came out to greet him, he hugged her and said, "I have gained the victory." She kissed him. Then they made ready to leave Kentucky and move to Missouri.

The search party came the next afternoon. Four horsemen rode up to the house and asked Jeroboam to come out. They told him he was under arrest and had to come back to Frankfort.

"What is the charge?" he asked.

"The murder of Colonel Sharp," he was told.

Jeroboam said he was innocent. He said he knew nothing of Sharp's death, but he agreed to go along without any trouble. The five of them left for Frankfort before dark. The second night they slept at an inn. One of the guards had brought the bloody bandanna to see if any of Jeroboam's neighbors could identify it. The guard was drinking and soon dropped off to sleep. During the night Jeroboam slipped the bandanna out of the guard's pocket and tossed it on the fire. Next morning no one could explain where it had gone.

On the fourth day the party reached Frankfort. While Jeroboam was kept under guard, a warrant was sworn out. It said that Jeroboam Beauchamp had stabbed and killed Solomon Sharp with a dagger on November 7 in Frankfort. An examining trial was held. Robert Scott, the owner of the boarding house, said he had rented a room to Jeroboam. Scott had heard Jeroboam get up and leave the house during the night. The city patrol said they had seen him near Sharp's house. The search party told how they had tracked Jeroboam to his farm and arrested him. The court found that Jeroboam should be tried for murder. Jeroboam asked that the trial be delayed until he could bring witnesses. His wish was granted. The trial was set for the second Monday in May 1826.

On that spring morning the streets were crowded.

There was much interest in the trial. The lawyers on both sides were among the best in Kentucky. When the judge was seated, the charges were read. The clerk then asked Jeroboam to answer guilty or not guilty.

"Not guilty," he said.

A jury was chosen, and the trial began. The first witness was Dr. Leander Sharp. He said that he had been called back to the Sharp house on the night of the murder. There he found his brother dying in a pool of blood. He described the wound as one inch wide and six inches deep. He thought it was caused by a butcher knife.

Mrs. Sharp took the stand wearing black. She described her husband opening the door for the killer. She said she saw Jeroboam stab her husband. She also recognized his "sharp, shrill voice." One of Jeroboam's neighbors said that Jeroboam had said he would kill Sharp.

A key witness was Patrick Darby, a political enemy of Sharp. Some people thought Darby had helped Jeroboam do the killing. Knowing he would be called, Darby had gone to Simpson County to gather evidence against Jeroboam. There he found a letter Jeroboam had written to his neighbor. The letter was read to the jury. It asked the neighbor, Captain John Low, to come to Frankfort to lie for Jeroboam to save him "from doom."

Then Jeroboam's witnesses took the stand. Though

many were called, they did little to help his case. The trial lasted about a week. After all the evidence was in, the lawyers made their closing statements. For two and a half days Jeroboam's lawyers argued that he was innocent. The Attorney General of Kentucky made the closing argument. When he finished, the jury went out to decide Jeroboam's fate.

After an hour the jurors came back. "We find the defendant, Jeroboam Beauchamp, guilty." They said he should be hanged. Jeroboam's lawyers asked that sentence not be announced until any case against his wife was decided. She had been charged with helping Jeroboam murder Sharp. Some witnesses were heard, and she was released. At the end of the day, she went back to the cell to be with Jeroboam. Though she was free, she wanted to stay with him.

On Monday morning Jeroboam was taken from his cell and marched to the courthouse. The judge sentenced him "to be hung by the neck until dead." The hanging was set for June 16, 1826.

When Jeroboam heard the sentence, he asked for more time. He wanted to write what happened in his own words. He wanted to explain why he had done what he had done. The judge granted his request, setting the date for July 7, six weeks later.

In his cell Jeroboam sat down to write his confession. In fact, he wrote two. The first was for his uncle. The second was for the public. Many believed the first was the more truthful of the two. In the second, Jeroboam painted himself as the hero of a romantic drama. He wanted to put the crime in a new light. He hoped the Governor would read it and pardon him. It ran 137 pages.

Jeroboam said he killed Sharp to make an example to those "who sport with innocence." He was punishing the father of Ann Cook's dead child. He declared himself a man of honor, not a murderer. But he had another purpose too. He wanted to persuade the Governor that he had not acted alone. If the Governor believed the killing was a plot by political enemies, he might grant Jeroboam a pardon.

To see justice done, Dr. Leander Sharp wrote his own account. He went to the Green River country where he took sworn statements from those close to the Beauchamps. He also described the Ann Beauchamp that he knew. In 1820 when he had met her, she was 33 or 34 years old. She was small, weighing about 90 pounds. She had dark hair and eyes. Her front teeth were gone. She was not very pretty and had a bad reputation.

Jeroboam and his wife lived in the cell six weeks. It was underground, had no windows, and was dimly lit. Food was brought down a ladder from a trap door. There was no way to escape.

On June 5, Jeroboam wrote the Governor to ask for a pardon. He said the trial had not been fair and promised to leave the country. Governor Desha did not answer. On July 4, Independence Day, Jeroboam wrote again. He asked to delay the hanging for 30 days. Jeroboam's uncle took the note to Governor Desha, who said he would not pardon Jeroboam. Nor would he delay the hanging.

A day or so before the hanging, the Governor ordered some units of the state militia to come to Frankfort. They were to guard the jail against those who would take the law into their own hands. They were also to escort Jeroboam to the hanging. At six o'clock that night Jeroboam and Ann heard a drum beating and asked what it meant. The jailor told them. It was clear to them both that Jeroboam was going to die. Ann decided to die with him.

On Friday morning Jeroboam had a message for the jailor. Ann had tried to end her life by taking a large dose of opium. Jeroboam had taken some too, but the only effect was to make them both sick. The two of them could still hear the drumming outside. Later, four ministers came to comfort Jeroboam. He sent them away, saying that his wife was ill. Before they left, he said he was ready to die. He asked them to come back at noon. He also asked them to join him on the ride to the gallows.

Again the Beauchamps tried to cheat the hangman. About an hour before the guards were to come, Jeroboam took out a small knife that he had hidden in the cell. He asked the guard to leave the room so his wife could dress. Halfway up the ladder, the guard heard a groan. Down he came. He found the two of them on the floor bleeding. Jeroboam told him that he and Ann were dying. He asked the guard to tell his parents that he and Ann were going straight to heaven. He said they had stabbed themselves.

The guard took the knife from Ann's hand. He saw a wound in her stomach. Jeroboam had a wound in his stomach too, but his was not so wide or so deep. The guard rushed out for help. Ann was carried out of the cell. She was placed in a room in the jailor's house. When asked about the stabbing, she said she had done it herself.

"I am dying for my dear husband," she said. The doctors said the wound would kill her.

The guards decided to hang Jeroboam before he died too. As he was taken from the cell, he asked to see Ann once more. He was told she was getting better. Going to her bed, he put out his hand to comfort her.

"Do you know me?" he asked. There was no answer.

"She's dying," he said. "You lied to me." He held her hand until she died. Then he kissed her and cried, "Farewell, child of sorrow. . . . For you I have lived, and for you I will die." He kissed her twice more and said he was ready to go.

At noon the soldiers marched outside the jailor's house. Behind them was a crowd, waiting to hear the news. A wagon drove up. On it was a coffin on which Jeroboam was expected to sit. Because he was so weak, he was put in a carriage instead. The jailor sat next to him. As they were about to go, Jeroboam asked to see Darby. He wanted to take back the lie he'd told about Darby's helping him. Darby came up but would not take Jeroboam's hand.

"This man is innocent," Jeroboam said, pointing toward Darby.

Then the drums started. The troops marched next to the carriage. It rolled up the hill and out of town. A large crowd followed. Some were riding, but most were walking. People were curious and wanted to hear what Jeroboam would say at the gallows. They wanted to see it all. Along the way were ladies watching from windows. Jeroboam waved to them.

When the carriage stopped, there were five or six thousand people on the hillside under the trees. Jeroboam looked at the gallows. He said the builder had done a good job. Saying good-bye, the jailor put a cover over his head.

By this time Jeroboam was so weak from loss of blood that he had to be lifted to sit on his coffin. He asked for a last drink of water. Then he asked the band to play a last tune. The name of it was "Bonaparte's

Retreat from Moscow." The water came, and he drank it. He asked the hangman to say when he was ready.

"All is ready," the hangman said. The rope was put around Jeroboam's neck. He stood up.

"Drive off," he said. "I'm ready to die." The wagon moved off, and he was left jumping in the air. He fought for about two minutes and then was still.

After a few minutes the body was taken down. It was given to his father, Thomas Beauchamp. His uncle came along to help. Together they loaded the bodies of Jeroboam and Ann onto a wagon. Then they drove to Bloomfield in Nelson County. They buried husband and wife in a single coffin with his right arm around her neck. A large stone was laid over the grave:

In Memory of
JEROBOAM O. BEAUCHAMP
Born Sept. 24th, 1802
and ANNA, his wife
Born Feb. 7th, 1786. Who both
left this world July 7th, 1826.

In the cell that last night Ann had written a poem. She asked that it be cut into the stone. These are the last lines:

Daughter of virtue moist thy tear,
This tomb of love and honor claim;

For thy defense the husband here,
Laid down in youth his life and fame.

His wife disdained a life forlorn,
Without her heart's lov'd, honor'd Loard.
Then reader, here their fortunes mourn,
Who for their love, their life blood pour'd.

A Frontier Tragedy

In 1807 Colonel Charles Lewis of Virginia and his sons made the most important decision of their lives. They decided to move their family to Kentucky to make a new start. The Lewises had been one of the richest families in Virginia. But in the years after the American Revolution, they had trouble making a living.

The first Lewis had come to Virginia from Wales in 1645. He became rich growing tobacco. His sons and daughters had married other well-to-do people. Charles himself had married Lucy Jefferson, the sister of Thomas Jefferson. Jefferson, who became third president of the United States, was a neighbor.

The Lewises were planters. Land, tobacco, and slaves had made them rich. They didn't do the work themselves but owned slaves who did it for them. Charles and his sons owned thousands of acres in Albemarle County in the western part of Virginia. Like many of their neighbors, they did not use the land well. They planted tobacco until the soil was used up. Then they bought more land and used that up. The Lewises did not rotate their crops. Nor did they let the fields lie fallow.

There was always land to the west. When more was needed, they bought it. The trees were cut down to plant new fields. When a son reached the age of 18 or so, his father would set him up as a planter. He

would give him some land and some slaves. Father
to son, father to son, this was the pattern they lived by.
This way of life was all they knew. There were few
schools since not much value was placed on education.
Charles, like his sons, learned reading, writing, and
simple arithmetic. None of them were educated to
become lawyers or doctors or teachers. None went into
business.

Girls in the family learned even less. They were
raised to marry well, have children, and run a
household. Daughters were married at 15 or 16, often
to close kin—a first or second cousin. In this way land
and money were kept in the family.

The Lewis men did not work with their hands.
Others worked for them. They hired a man to manage
their crops and work their slaves. They spent most of
the time enjoying themselves. They loved to hunt and
took pride in the fine horses they bred. Since no large
cities were close by, they spent time close to home.
They joined the state militia, which was a part-time
army of citizens. They also entered local politics. They
intermarried to protect their wealth.

Charles Lewis married Lucy Jefferson in 1769. At
the time, her brother Thomas was building Monticello,
his home near Charlottesville. During the American
Revolution, which lasted from 1775 to 1781, Charles
served as a colonel in the county militia. At the end of
the war he owned 40 adult slaves and 3,000 acres of
farmland. In addition to three daughters, he had four

sons—Randolph, Lilburne, Charles, and Isham. When Randolph and Lilburne came of age, they married sisters who were their second cousins. These older sons set up farms in partnership with their father. There was little their father could do for Charles and Isham, the younger sons.

Times changed. Money was tight after the Revolution, and crops failed. Tobacco had used up the soil so that land was not worth much. Other fields were planted in wheat or corn year after year. The weather and insects damaged the harvest. The Lewises found themselves with land they couldn't use, little money, and many mouths to feed. Their debts grew. To pay them, they had to sell off land and rent out or sell their slaves. More money was going out than coming in. They borrowed more money and sold off more land until they were nearly broke. There was personal tragedy too. The younger son Charles had joined the army and died of fever in Louisiana.

The family held a meeting to discuss their future. Randolph, the eldest brother, was a big man, hard-working and serious. Lilburne was next in age, restless and very ambitious. Both brothers owned their own land but were having a hard time making it pay. Lilburne was first to bring up the idea of moving.

"You know," he said, "I'm tempted to sell out and move to Kentucky. Others have done it and made out fine."

Colonel Lewis liked the idea. "They tell me," the

old man said, "a man can clear enough to pay for his land with three good crops." Moving west for new land was nothing new to the Lewises. It was what they had always done.

Lilburne already saw himself owning Eden as far as he could see, a green empire. "Let's go then," he said. "There's nothing for us here. Why not start out new in a new place? We can pack what we need and sell off the rest. With the money we can buy more land than we could ever hope to own here—better land too."

From the first Colonel Lewis was won over, but Randolph was slower to come around. He was more careful, slower to act. He wanted to talk about the risks they would take.

"What if things go bust?" he asked. "What if the crops are bad or we get in over our heads?"

"Then we'll be no worse off than we are now," Lilburne said. "I'm for going, the sooner the better. I'd rather go bust for a fortune than starve out here, acre by acre, teaspoon by teaspoon."

Colonel Lewis agreed and so did his wife, Lucy, though she hated to leave the people and place she'd known all her life. Still, she saw the sense of what her husband and Lilburne were saying. Besides, when they were settled, she could come back to visit. Randolph finally gave in too, and it was agreed to prepare to go as soon as possible.

So in 1807 the Lewises made ready to move to

Kentucky for a new start. All three families decided to go. Only Isham, the youngest, chose to stay. His brothers were able to sell their land in Virginia. Colonel Lewis sold what he had left too. They held back what they needed to set up a new life—tools, furniture, and farm animals. West of the mountains was Eden. They wanted to see it for themselves. Land there was fertile and cheap, full of wild game and timber.

The Lewises were not alone. Many others were making the same choice for the same reasons. Randolph and Lilburne got good prices for their farms. With the money they bought as much Kentucky land as they could. The cheapest was farthest west. It lay along the Ohio River in Livingston County. Lilburne bought 1,500 acres for $8,300. Randolph bought 3,833 acres for $9,100. This was more than he needed, but he planned to sell some of it for profit. Colonel Lewis had no money to spend on land. He and his wife planned to go along because they had no other place to go. They wanted to live out their old age with their children and grandchildren. There was nothing left for any of them in Virginia.

With high hopes the Lewises set out for Kentucky on November 20, 1807. In all there were 40 people. There were six adults, 15 children from infants to teenagers, and 20 or so slaves. Also, there were horses, cattle, hogs, and sheep. The Lewises took tools, plows, and furniture. They carried everything needed to build a new home in the West. At Pittsburgh, a rough town on the Ohio, they bought a flatboat to float down the river. It was large enough to hold all of them and their belongings. At the end of the trip they planned to break up the boat and use the wood for their houses.

The journey was not easy. The distance from Albemarle County to their new home was 1,180 miles, most of it by water. They started late in the year when the weather was against them. In the Ohio were snags and tricky currents. Along parts of it there were pirates. Indians were known to shoot people as they floated past the wooded shore.

Their trip should have taken five weeks but instead took ten. Winter slowed them. The river was a wide gray ribbon. Trees on the bluffs were like needles, leafless and gray. Sometimes they saw a cabin with its thread of smoke. Sickness or ice on the Ohio forced them to lay over. They had to pass the Falls of the Ohio at Louisville, the largest town. It was a cluster of wood and brick buildings along muddy streets.

When they came to Livingston County at last, they found no Eden. Instead there was wilderness, a vast forest of rolling uplands. The bottomland was filled with cane. There were few roads, few neighbors. In the county were several towns. The county seat was Centreville. It had a log courthouse and two taverns. About 40 whites and six slaves lived there. Most people were living on isolated farms cut out of the wilderness.

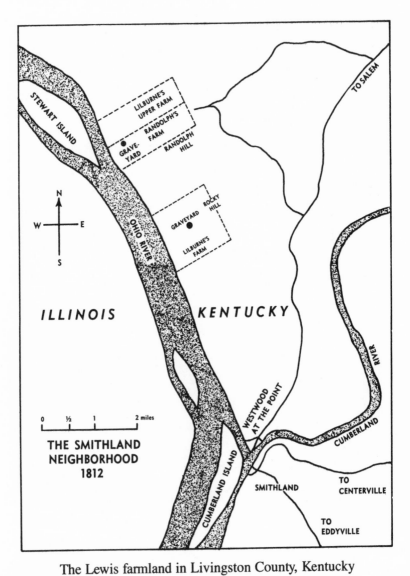

The Lewis farmland in Livingston County, Kentucky

Map by Thomas E. Clark from *Jefferson's Nephews: A Frontier Tragedy*, 2d edition, by Boynton Merrill, Jr.

When the Lewises came to Livingston County, Kentucky had been a state for 15 years. The first settlers had come 30 years before. Parts of the county were cleared. There were markets and more farms down the river. There was some law and order—a jail, a sheriff, and traveling judges. The Indians had been pushed north of the Ohio River.

For the first time in their lives, Lilburne and Randolph had a great deal of work to do. They and their slaves had to clear enough land to build houses and plant a crop. Only four or five of the slaves were able to do field work, and the brothers had to work hard too. They had few tools and only crude wooden plows to break the new ground. Yet they planted a crop of corn and wheat. They put in vegetables for the table. They also built fairly large houses. The flatboat gave them some lumber, but they bought more at a nearby sawmill.

Lilburne built his house on a hill overlooking the rear of his farm. He called it Rocky Hill. A smaller house was built for his parents near Randolph's. Most of the furniture for the three houses came from Virginia. By the end of the first year there were signs that the family would succeed in their new home.

But starting in April of 1809 things went wrong. Lilburne's wife Elizabeth died in childbirth, as did the baby. She was only 27 years old. Lilburne was left with five children to care for. The youngest was two, the oldest 11. He loved Elizabeth very deeply and was lost without her. She was buried at a spot near the top of Rocky Hill.

To add to his troubles, that summer his children and slaves were often sick. Some were down with malaria, and Lilburne had to send for a doctor. There were money troubles too. The farm had no income. He owed the doctor. He had sent two of his daughters to school in Lexington and could not pay the bills. Some of the people he owed took him to court. Just at this time his mother became very sick.

There was also bad news from far away. One of the Lewis cousins, Meriwether Lewis, took his own life in western Tennessee. He was one of the two leaders of the famous Lewis and Clark expedition to explore the land bought in the Louisiana Purchase of 1803. Thomas Jefferson had bought the land from France and selected Lewis to lead the expedition. President Jefferson said the cause of death was depression that ran in the Lewis family.

Despite these problems, Lilburne and Randolph did their best. They became active in the community. Both of them served on the grand jury for county court. They met their neighbors and came to know local leaders. Lilburne was chosen by the court to settle a legal dispute. There was still some threat from Indians from just across the river. So the brothers joined the militia, and Lilburne became a captain. When the troops mustered, Lilburne put on a fancy uniform with a sword and wore a feather in his hat. Randolph was chosen as supervisor of the county roads. The Lewises were Presbyterians and joined the local church.

And there was news from the youngest brother, Isham. He had stayed in Virginia when the family came to Kentucky. He came for a visit on his way home from a trip to St. Louis. He stayed with his family for a short time. Then he left for Mississippi where he hoped to find work.

The money problems grew worse. Lilburne could not pay his debts. In 1810 he owned 14 slaves, but only seven lived at Rocky Hill. The rest were rented out to other farms, not leaving him enough help to run his own farm. Soon he came up with the idea of forming his own town. It was to be called Westwood and would be built on land he owned near the river. He had plans drawn up and put up lots for sale. But there were no buyers. He then got a job as census-taker during 1810. The money helped, but it was not enough. Randolph's problems were the same. He had much land but little income. Of the seven slaves he owned, only two were grown men and both were rented out. He also tried to sell off some land, but there were no buyers.

Then after a long illness their mother, Lucy, died. She had been the mainstay of the family, loved and respected by all. She was buried on the high hill above the Ohio. Without her, Colonel Lewis was helpless.

He too had debts he could not pay. He had to rely on his children who themselves had very little. The family was just scraping by.

About this time Lilburne began courting "the belle of the county." Her name was Letitia Rutter. In November of 1811 he married her, and she came to live at Rocky Hill. Her family had power in the county. Soon after the marriage, Lilburne and Randolph were proposed as justices of the peace. Randolph won the appointment. But just at this time his health began to fail. At the same time, Isham returned from Mississippi sick with malaria. The family was in trouble. Deaths, debts, and illness had all but defeated them. They had come to Kentucky with dreams, but those dreams were fading. Still they tried to find a way to fulfill their hopes.

Then Randolph died, leaving a wife and eight children with no means of support. He was only 38 years old. His property had to be sold. With his brother gone and his father growing old, Lilburne became head of the Lewis families. Though he had a new wife, he didn't know if they could make it. He was under great stress. Letitia, his new wife, was soon pregnant. His debts were still growing. Depressed, he started to drink. When he drank, he was often quick to anger.

The year 1811 was not a good one for other Kentuckians. There was a flood early in the year. In April a comet crossed the skies. Lack of rain that summer dried up many of the crops in western Kentucky. In September there was an almost total eclipse of the sun. Many read this as a bad omen. The great Shawnee chief Tecumseh was uniting the Indians to drive out the whites and reclaim their lost land. In November the chief's brother led an attack against a party of whites to the north. The Indians were beaten, but many Kentuckians died there. It was learned that the British had supplied the Indians with guns. The year ended with an earthquake at New Madrid, the greatest on record in North America. Many saw the shaking of earth as a sign that God was coming to punish the wicked. Finally, this was the year of the undoing of the Lewises.

Lilburne owned a slave named George, who worked around the house as a servant and errand boy. At 17 he was tall and gangly. He had an ugly scar over one eye. Lilburne was said to be fair but firm with his slaves, but he and George did not get along. George tried to keep away from him, especially when Lilburne was drinking. In early December George ran off for a few days. When he came back to Rocky Hill, Lilburne had it in for him.

"Where were you off to this time?" he demanded.

George mumbled an answer and wouldn't say. He knew nothing he could say would make things better.

Lilburne took a pitcher out of the cupboard and put it on the table. The pitcher was white with a blue pattern of plump birds fluttering around little trees. Lilburne prized it. The pitcher had belonged to Lucy before she and Charles were married.

"George, I want you to take this pitcher down to the spring and fetch me some water." George nodded but said nothing. "You hear me?"

"Yes sir, Mr. Lilburne." He took up the pitcher and walked over to the door.

"And mind you don't break it."

"No sir, I won't break it."

With that he left the house. About ten minutes later he came back without the pitcher.

"Well," Lilburne said, "where's my water?"

"I couldn't get any," George said. He was staring at the floor, scared.

"What happened that you couldn't fetch the water? Was there ice in the spring?"

"No sir, there wasn't any ice."

"Well, what was it then?" said Lilburne, beginning to get mad and lifting the half-empty bottle from the table.

"I was coming back up the hill and slipped on a rock and dropped it," George said. "I was carrying it careful as I could, and it just dropped out of my hands. I didn't mean to do it, and I'm awful sorry."

"Sorry isn't good enough," Lilburne yelled. He glared at George for a minute. "Get out to the kitchen," he said, "and wait till I come out."

"Yes sir," George said and backed out the door. He turned and walked slowly to the kitchen house.

Lilburne called to Isham. The two of them then went out to the kitchen cabin, which sat to the rear of the main house. With Isham's help, Lilburne tied George's hands behind his back. He then sent Isham off to round up the other slaves. Lilburne ordered two of the slaves to build up a big fire in the fireplace. Isham bolted the door. When the fire was roaring, Lilburne faced George and the others. Most of them, sensing a punishment, would not look him in the eye.

"This time I'm going to teach you all a lesson," he said, "a lesson you won't forget."

"Kneel down," he ordered George. George knelt down before him, too scared to speak.

"Lilburne, what are you going to do?" Isham asked, realizing for the first time that his brother was going too far.

"Never you mind," said Lilburne. "Just watch."

With that he took up the ax that lay against the woodbox. He raised it over his head and swung it down on George. The sharp edge struck George's neck with a thunk and killed him instantly. Terrified, everyone looked on, not wanting to believe what they had seen.

Blood was pouring out of the wound. George was dead without uttering a sound. Putting the ax aside, Lilburne ordered one of the slaves to cut up George's body and burn it in the fire. Shaking, the man did what he was told. When he finished, Lilburne gave everyone a warning.

"If any of you tell anyone about this," he said, "as God is my witness, I'll kill you." Then he sent them off to bed. Calmer now, Lilburne had no guilt. He felt safe because the law said slaves could not give evidence against their masters in court. He did not worry about Isham. Saying goodnight to him, Lilburne went off to bed. This was on Sunday, December 14, 1811.

At two o'clock that morning everyone was awakened by a shock. The ground shook and china fell off the shelves. Everything was still a moment and then started to shake again. Lilburne and Letitia ran out of the house. Next morning they found that the chimney of the kitchen had fallen in. Lilburne said nothing to Letitia, though he knew the remains of George were in the ashes. All that Monday the ground shook. When it stopped, they slept in the house again. A few days later Lilburne ordered the chimney rebuilt.

For a time life went on as usual at Rocky Hill. There were some aftershocks of the earthquake but none so strong as the first night. Soon Letitia gave birth to a baby boy. When she asked about George, she was told he had run off. Lilburne kept all his slaves as close to home as possible. He didn't want word about George to leak out, though he must have known he couldn't keep the killing a secret for long.

There was more bad news when Randolph's widow died. She left eight children, five of them under the age of 12.

Early in February the earth shook again. Again, the chimney came down. The unburned bones of George were in the ashes. Lilburne had a dog named Nero. Unknown to his master, Nero carried off George's skull. A neighbor who was passing saw Nero chewing what looked like a human head. He got it away from Nero and took it to the sheriff. The sheriff came out to ask questions. He questioned everyone on the place and learned that George was missing.

A grand jury was formed. After hearing the facts, the jury indicted Lilburne and Isham for murder. Under the law the punishment for murder was death. The news rocked Livingston County like another earthquake. A warrant was taken out to arrest Lilburne. He was ordered to appear before the court and answer the charges. A second grand jury was called to charge Isham. Both brothers were taken to jail to await the next term of court. Lilburne's bail was set at $1,000, Isham's at $500. The brothers made bail and were released. If they did not appear on a certain date, the money would be taken out of their property and paid to the court.

Lilburne and Isham, free from jail, went back to

Rocky Hill. Letitia knew about the murder by then and was afraid to stay under the same roof with her husband. Under the law she could not give evidence against him, but she could against Isham. After Isham was indicted, she decided to leave. Taking her baby son, she went back to her family. Her brothers came along to protect her. Lilburne begged her to stay, but she went anyway.

This left Lilburne alone at Rocky Hill with only his brother Isham for company. His mother was dead. His first wife was dead. His second wife had deserted him. His own children were at his father's. Randolph's family and his father were dependent on him. He had debts he couldn't pay. He had also lost his standing in the community. In a fit of anger, he had taken a boy's life. He had felt no guilt. Now his wife was afraid to live with him. Even his neighbors were afraid. Accused of murder, he would soon stand trial and be judged by them. He had lost his self-respect, his reason for living. His coming to Kentucky had ended in failure and death. He was an outcast, and he needed a way out.

In early April Lilburne decided to kill himself. He talked with Isham, and together they made plans to commit suicide. On Thursday, the ninth of April, Lilburne wrote his will. He wanted his property to be divided among his children. To his "cruel wife Letitia" he left only what the law gave her. To his father went his riding horse and hunting rifle. His dog Nero was to go to his father too. He also left money to bring charges of trespass against Letitia's family. Against his wishes her brothers had come on the farm and taken her home. On the back of the will was a note to his lawyer:

Rocky Hill Apl. 9, 1812. Mr. James McCawley I have fallen a victim to my beloved but cruel wife Letitia. I die in the hope of being united to my other wife in Heaven. Take care of this Will & come here that we may be decently buried. Adieu. L. Lewis

On Friday the sky was cloudy and gray. There was no sun. Parts of the river bottom were flooded. Lilburne and Isham climbed up Rocky Hill to the graveyard. Lilburne told Isham that he wanted to lie close to his first wife. Each of the brothers carried a rifle. When they reached the top, they looked out over the pale ridges that stretched far as the eye could see. Below was the river snaking into the hills, its water glowing like the blade of a knife. Lilburne, who had brought along the will, put it under a small stone so it wouldn't blow away.

"How are we going to do it?" Isham asked.

"It's simple," said Lilburne. "We stand facing each other. We'll point our guns at each other's chests. When all is ready, on the count of three we'll pull our triggers."

"But what if the gun misfires?" Isham said.

Lilburne hadn't thought about this, and he took some time to answer.

"Well," he said, "if something goes wrong, you can do it yourself."

"But how?"

Lilburne looked around and picked up a stick about as long as his arm. Next he sat down, resting his back against the gravestone. He cocked his rifle. Then he turned the muzzle toward his own chest.

"It's simple," he said. "Just aim the rifle with one hand and use the other to trip the trigger." As Isham looked on, Lilburne took up the stick and stuck it in the trigger guard.

The stillness was broken by a tremendous bang, and Lilburne slumped over, his white shirt covered with blood. Before the sound had faded in the hills, Isham knew his brother was dead. Shocked by the blood, Isham could not turn his rifle on himself. He couldn't lift it. He couldn't move. The shot brought Lilburne's slaves running up the hill. There they found their master dead.

Several days later an inquest was held. Isham told how Lilburne shot himself by accident. Still, a warrant was issued to arrest Isham. The charge was helping Lilburne to take his own life. So Isham was jailed to await his trial. Sometime before that day, he escaped. Never again was he seen in Livingston County, and a legend grew around his disappearance. He had gone south to New Orleans. Two years later he was killed by the British during the Battle of New Orleans. There were six Americans who died, and the story goes that he was one of them.

In 1808 the Lewises, proud and confident, had come to Kentucky to make a new start. Four years later, only the oldest adult was alive. Colonel Charles Lewis was left with 13 grandchildren and three unmarried daughters. Unable to care for them, he gave up control to the county court. Guardians were appointed for the youngest children. The family was broken up and its property sold at public auction. The tragedy of the Lewises was complete.

The Battle of Blue Licks

On the night of August 15, 1782, a party of British and
Indians surrounded the tiny settlement of Bryan's
Station five miles north of Lexington, Kentucky. They
had crossed the Ohio at the mouth of the Licking River
and followed the buffalo trail south. No one knew they
were coming, and they gave no warning. Sixty or so
British rangers were led by Captain William Caldwell.
The Indians, several hundred of them, were Wyandots.
With them was Simon Girty, the most hated man in
Kentucky. As a teenager, Girty had been captured by
the Indians. He had learned their language and ways.
When the American Revolution started, it was natural
for him to side with the Indians.

Before the raid Girty made a speech to the Indians,
urging them to fight. "Brothers," he said, "the Long
Knives have destroyed the cane, trodden down the
clover, killed the deer and the buffalo, the beaver and
the raccoon. If you do not drive them off, you will lose
the hunting grounds of your fathers." Stirred by his
words, several hundred vowed they would kill all the
whites in Kentucky.

Outside Bryan's Station these Indians hid in the
cane, hoping to kill the settlers when they came out for
their morning chores. Inside the fort were only 44 men
and their families. They knew that Indians had attacked

another station close by. In fact, they planned to go help their neighbors in the morning.

After dawn a Negro slave named Jim stepped out of the gate between the log walls. The Indians fired on him, alerting the settlers to the danger. Those inside quickly made ready to defend themselves. Their leader, Captain John Craig, sent two riders to Lexington for help. Hoping to hide their numbers, the Indians did not fire on them.

The fort's source of water was a spring outside the walls. After much debate, the settlers decided to pretend they did not know the Indians were there. Some of the women and slaves went out to milk the cows, kneeling to pray before they left. A second group went to the spring, talking and laughing as if they were not aware of the Indians. By a clump of bushes someone saw a hand holding a tomahawk. But everything went well. They made it back carrying pails of water. Caldwell and Girty kept their men from firing. They were still hoping to catch a large number of fighting men in the open. There was only the sound of a few birds as both sides waited in silence.

Captain Craig wanted to know how many of the enemy there were and where they were hidden. He hit upon the plan of sending some men outside as decoys. Thirteen agreed to ride out and draw the Indians' fire. At about eight o'clock the gates of the fort were opened, and 13 riders showed themselves. The Indians fired and came charging out from the trees and bushes. Led by Simon Girty, they raised a loud yell and rushed toward the log walls. But Craig and the others were ready. At just the right moment, they fired. A great cry went up, and the Indians ran for cover, leaving several dead outside the walls. They came back later and set fire to five cabins outside the fort. They cut down much of the corn and burned the hemp that was standing. They pulled up potatoes. Then they killed 300 hogs, 150 cattle, and a number of sheep. They also stole as many horses as they could catch. Flaming arrows hit roofs of cabins inside the fort, but several small boys climbed up and poured water on the fires. One arrow struck the cradle of a baby named Richard Mentor Johnson, who later became ninth vice-president of the United States.

The two riders sent out by Craig went straight to Lexington where they raised the alarm. Word spread over the countryside, to Harrodsburg and as far as Stanford in Lincoln County. At two in the afternoon 40 men under Major Levi Todd arrived from Lexington. Some were on horseback, some on foot. To reach the fort, they had to pass a large cornfield. From it the Indians fired on them. With the first shots, those on horseback rushed safely to the fort. They were partly hidden by clouds of dust on the dry trail. Those on foot were not so lucky. Fighting their way through the corn stalks, they lost two men before they reached the fort.

By nightfall the Indians were let down. Their plans had failed. There was no surprise, no success in rushing the fort, no fire to burn it down. They had lost men—five killed and two wounded. Time was against them, and they wanted to leave while they could. Simon Girty tried to do with words what he couldn't do with guns. Creeping up behind a large stump outside the fort, he yelled to those inside.

"There are 600 men against you," he shouted, "and more are on the way. They are bringing cannon to blow your walls down."

There was silence.

"What I am saying is true," Girty assured them, "as certain as my name is Simon Girty."

Another silence.

"What is the matter? Don't you know me?" Girty shouted.

Then up rose Aaron Reynolds, a young man known for his swearing. He had climbed inside a stone chimney, and only his head was showing. "The name Simon Girty is well known to all of us," he shouted. "I myself own two good-for-nothing dogs, one named Simon and the other Girty. If more of you are coming, come on and be damned. If you and your gang of murderers are here tomorrow, your scalps will be found drying under the roofs of our cabins."

Disappointed, Girty sneaked back to the Indians. Caldwell, Girty, and the chiefs met that night and decided to leave. There was firing during the night, but it stopped before dawn. By ten o'clock that morning the Indians had left camp.

During the day help poured in from the surrounding settlements. Colonel Stephen Trigg brought men from Harrodsburg. Colonel Daniel Boone and his son Israel came from Boone's Station. Colonel John Todd, Levi's brother, had arrived to take command of the men from Fayette County. Though only 30 years old, he was one of the most respected men in the country. He was the only man who carried a sword. Among the other officers were Majors Silas Harlan and an Irishman named Hugh McGary. Altogether there were about 180 men. They knew that Colonel Benjamin Logan would join them within a day, bringing a larger force with them. All of them wanted revenge, to punish the Indians so they would not soon come back. The question now was what to do—wait or follow.

That night the officers held a meeting in John Craig's cabin. John and Levi Todd were on hand, as were Stephen Trigg, Daniel Boone, Hugh McGary, Silas Harlan, and four or five others. John Todd and Trigg did most of the talking.

"As I see it," said Todd, "we must choose between waiting for Ben Logan to arrive sometime late tomorrow or starting in the morning so we can chase down the

Indians before they cross the Ohio. I say we should go now and let Logan catch up."

"Whoa," said Hugh McGary. "I want to see the devils pay too. But let's not be foolish. Since we don't know how many there are, the wisest thing might be to wait for Logan."

"What makes you think they'll wait for Logan?" said Stephen Trigg. He was the commander of the militia in Lincoln County. At six feet two inches, he was the tallest man in the room.

"I can't promise that they won't run," said McGary. "But a body of Indians this large can't move as fast and doesn't need to."

"Yes," said Todd, "but if we don't leave soon we might lose them. A single day is all they need to cross the river and be home scot-free."

"But there are more of them," McGary said, "than there are of us."

"We don't know that," said Trigg. "You know how easy it is to see one feather and count a dozen." Several of the others nodded in agreement. "The best time to hit them is when they're in one body, and that's just what I mean to do."

"Colonel Trigg is right," said Todd. "Make them pay dearly for their trip this time and there may not be another. Waiting is for cowards."

This angered McGary, who knew that Todd was coming close to calling him a coward. He told himself he'd done his best to reason with them. Now he would go along. When the time came, he would prove himself. He was sorry that Boone, the one whose advise would weigh heaviest, said nothing. Through it all, the older man sat looking into the fire. No one asked his advice, and he didn't give it.

One-hundred and eighty men left Bryan's Station on the morning of August 18, going north as fast as their horses would carry them. The weather was sultry, the trail dusty. By mid-morning horses and men were drenched with sweat. The path of the Indians was easy to follow. Trees along the buffalo trail were blazed with tomahawks. But numbers were hard to know since the Indians played their old trick of having each man follow in the steps of the one ahead. Reaching the place where Caldwell had camped the night before, Todd and his officers realized that McGary was right. Caldwell's force was larger than they had guessed. Boone counted their fires and said there were at least 500 Indians.

At dusk they rested and ate the cold food their women had packed at Bryan's Station. Todd called a meeting again to form a plan. This time there was no debate. Half of the men on horseback were to ride hard to catch up. The others would follow as fast as they could. All of them now believed they could beat the Indians if they could only catch them. Chances were good since only a few of the Indians had horses. All of Todd's men did. They rode half the night before setting up camp. They had gone about 33 miles. After putting out some guards, they slept. Though neither side knew it, the two camps were sleeping about three miles apart.

The horsemen were up at dawn and off again soon after. They continued to gain on the Indians, who traveled as though they had nothing to fear from those behind them. By this time the pursuit was close to the Lower Blue Licks of the Licking River. The more Boone saw, the more he didn't like it. He had the feeling they were being drawn into an ambush.

Ahead of them lay the Licking River. The road crossed at a horseshoe bend in the river, which was shallow enough to ford. On the other side was a swampy bottom and a steep hill with a barren top, a place where buffalo had eaten or stamped down all the trees and brush. At the top were two ravines full of cane and fallen timber. The country around was craggy and wild.

Daniel Boone, who was then 50, was the most experienced woodsman among the settlers. He had been captured by Shawnees near this very spot in 1776. He, like the buffalo, had come for the salt at the nearby springs. The narrow trail through the woods had been cut by thousands of buffalo over hundreds, maybe thousands, of years. He knew the lay of the land, especially that this place was perfect for an ambush. Attackers had to climb the hill, and there was no cover

Daniel Boone

when they reached the top. Indians in the ravines had cover and an easy means of retreat. If the attackers retreated, they had to recross the river that nearly encircled them.

When the Kentuckians reached the south side of the Licking, they could see Indians moving slowly up the ridge on the north side. Some turned boldly and looked back at the newcomers. Colonel John Todd, the commander, sent for Boone. He wanted to draw on Boone's experience with the Indians. Boone had lived with them and knew their ways.

"What will the Indians do if we cross the river?" Todd asked him.

"They will fight," said Boone. He explained that the Indians were likely hiding in the ravines beyond the top of the hill.

"What would you suggest we do?" Todd asked.

Boone thought a full minute before answering. "I would cross the river higher up," he said, "and then strike the trace again on the high ground to the north." Doing this, they both knew, would take them around any ambush at this spot.

Good as this advice was, no one seemed ready to follow it. Boone was overruled, and some of the riders made their way down the ridge to the ford of the river. Before they reached the water, Colonel Todd called a halt. He still wanted to discuss what course of action to take.

It was now about eight o'clock in the morning. At this point the little army was in three columns. Todd called his commanders together again—Boone, Trigg, and Harlan. McGary and several other officers were on hand too. All of them believed that Colonel Logan was following not too far behind. They would prefer to have him with them, but they knew the Indians would not wait much longer. Again Boone said he was worried about crossing. He recommended that they wait until Logan and his men were with them.

While this was going on, Todd sent two scouts across the river to see if there were Indians ahead. The commanders looked on as the two riders splashed into the Licking. In some places the water rose above their horses' necks. When the horses found the riverbed again, they scrambled up the banks. The scouts, once again on solid ground, followed the buffalo trace up the hill where they dropped out of sight. A few minutes later they rode back down and crossed again. They reported that there were no signs of Indians.

"Sign or no sign," Boone said, "I tell you there are 300 to 500 Indians waiting for us in the ravines." He knew the ground, and he knew Indians.

"What would you have us do, then?" Todd asked. "Should we simply sit here waiting for Logan until they slip away?"

Boone said there was no need for that. Instead, they should split into two forces. One would move upstream and cross at the next ford and attack one of the ravines from the side. The other force would attack from another direction. Todd and several others were impressed with the common sense of Boone's advice. They were prepared to follow it when Major Hugh McGary came forward. McGary was from North Carolina, and his wife was one of the first three white women to come to Kentucky. Still smarting from the hint that he was a coward, he wanted to prove himself.

"I say let's cross right here and hit them while we can hurt them. By the time we split and cross, the whole kit and caboodle will be gone."

Boone tried another argument. "This ford is the worst place to cross," he warned. His sharp eyes were scanning the slopes on the other side of the river. "If we must cross," he said, "let's cross downstream where the ford is not so deep."

"How far is that?" McGary shot back. His big bay horse was stepping nervously by the water's edge. McGary's rifle was slung across his saddle, at the ready.

"About two miles," Boone said.

McGary grumbled something about this ford being good enough for anyone who wanted to fight.

Boone was quick to set him straight. "If you must go fight the enemy from this place," he said, "go on. I can go as far as any man in a fight."

McGary in the river at the Battle of Blue Licks

This was enough talk for McGary. Swinging his horse around, he rode down the bank and plunged into the water. He turned in the saddle and raised his rifle above his head, shouting, "Let all who are not cowards follow me, and I will show you where the Indians are!"

There was a pause, each man wanting to see how the others would react. Todd was speechless. Boone stood nodding his head and looking at the ground. But all were proud men, confident of their abilities. They had been challenged. Several of the officers were already mounting their horses and heading down the bank.

Then all of them, officers and men, spurred their horses down the bank into the water. The three columns melted into one as they streamed across the

Licking and formed on the north bank. When all were across, Todd called another halt to plan the attack.

Boone was to lead one column on the left. Trigg was to lead one on the right. Colonel Todd, riding his white horse, kept the center for himself. At this point many of the men leaped down from their horses to fight on foot. The horses were left untied. Majors Silas Harlan and McGary with Captain William McBride were to lead 25 horsemen ahead of the main body to feel out the enemy.

Moving up to the top of the ridge where the first Indians had been seen, the advance riders had no trouble. They then moved forward toward one of the ravines. When they were about 50 yards away, there was a roar of gunfire from the trees. From the ravines came a series of flashes. All but three of the riders toppled off their horses. The leaders, Harlan and Trigg, were among the dead. McGary was one of the survivors.

By this time Colonel Todd and the main army had reached the top of the ridge. They went forward to aid the advance guard. There was no cover. The men started firing into the trees by the ravines where they could see little wads of smoke like cotton. The guns were popping from the woods. By twos and threes they fell dead or wounded. In less than three minutes, 40 of Todd's men were down, almost a fourth of the whole army.

Boone led his men forward on the left, reaching one
ravine and pushing the Indians back a hundred yards or
so. He could see Indians dodging from tree to tree.
Raising his rifle to his shoulder, he fired and saw one of
them go down. Trigg was moving up on the right when
his line was hit by fire from the Indians hidden ahead of
him. Trigg himself was one of the first to fall, shot
through the side. In the confusion, his men drew back.
As the firing picked up, they darted for cover. The
Indians kept up a steady fire, turning the right flank
back on the center. Todd's men, still out in front,
started taking fire on the right side as well as the
center. Todd himself was already dead from a ball in
the left side of his chest. The others saw that the
Indians were about to encircle them.

Boone was holding his own on the left. Early in the
battle, Boone had grabbed a stray horse, telling his son
Israel to get away while he could.

"Father, I won't leave you!" he shouted, and raised
his rifle to fire. Boone heard a shot and turned to find
his son lying on the ground, blood coming out of his
mouth. Knowing he was badly wounded, Boone picked
him up and carried him to a safe place. He hoped to
hide him where the Indians would not find him. Not
being able to do more, he went back to lead his men.
He found them nearly surrounded and told them to fall
back. Yard by yard, tree by tree, he led them off to the
left toward the river. They followed the high ground
until the shooting seemed far away. Then they went

down to the river. They were able to swim it safely nearly two miles from where they had first crossed. None of the Indians had followed.

Things did not go so well back with the main body of men. Seeing that things were in their favor, the Indians threw down their rifles. They raised a victory shout, running out of the cane swinging their tomahawks and scalping knives. Some of them mounted horses whose owners had been shot.

Panic now swept over the Kentuckians. Most of their leaders were dead, and the Indians were charging out of the woods. Many fired a last shot and dashed for the river, each man for himself. Most of those killed during the battle died trying to cross the water. Many were caught at the water's edge. Some were shot as they slogged across. Others fell as they tried to scale the cliffs. A few even drowned. The ford was shallow enough, but the water to either side was deep. It was not long before the greenish water ran red.

One of the first to reach the other side was Benjamin Netherland, a veteran of the war in the East. He was on a horse and could have raced away. Instead, he turned and ordered a body of horsemen coming up behind him to halt and shoot over the heads of those in the water. "Let's give them a fire," he shouted. Twenty or so of the riders stopped and emptied their rifles into the Indians on the other shore. Some of the closest fell. Others ducked behind trees. This gave those in the water enough time to reach safety.

There was another act of heroism at the ford. Aaron Reynolds was about to cross to safety when he saw one of the officers, Robert Patterson, who needed help. He jumped down from his horse and helped Patterson into the saddle. "Get on," he yelled, "and make your escape." Patterson was able to cross the river and get away, racing past two Indians who were standing behind a tree. He was the last to make it over safely. Reynolds swam across but had to take off his wet buckskin trousers in order to run. While doing so, he was captured by three Indians. Two of them left to chase someone else. Guarded by one Indian, Reynolds was able to knock the man down and run into the woods. He made it back to Bryan's Station wearing only his hunting shirt.

As the other survivors came out of the water, they scattered into the trees. Some of the Indians also crossed, chasing the Kentuckians nearly two miles. But most were busy taking scalps and picking up rifles and other valuables left on the battlefield. Before leaving to cross the Ohio, they stripped, scalped, and cut up all the dead. The battle had lasted about 15 minutes.

The British Captain Caldwell was very pleased with the outcome. Only 14 of his men were wounded and ten killed. As for the Kentuckians, 67 men had lost their lives. Many of them were officers, including Todd, Trigg, Harlan, and McBride. Seven men were captured, four of them later tortured to death. This brought the final count to 71 dead.

Colonel Benjamin Logan and his militia finally reached the site of the battle. They had marched from Bryan's Station and along the way heard the news from survivors. From them they learned the names of many who had died. Logan took the survivors back to Bryan's Station. Daniel Boone's nephew, Squire Boone, Jr., rode all the way back from the battle with a broken thigh. Five days later Logan returned to Blue Licks with 500 men to bury the dead. Before they reached the battlefield, they saw a great wheel of turkey buzzards circling high above the site. They crossed the river and started gathering the bodies. Most they could not recognize. The dead were cut up and bloated from the heat. Some had been eaten by wild animals. Logan's men buried the remains in a common grave.

Kentucky lost many of its most promising leaders at Blue Licks. It was the worst military defeat during the state's early history. As Boone later said, "Many widows were now made." The country was full of orphans. The causes were failure of judgment, over-confidence, and a willingness to take chances. Stephen Trigg, Silas Harlan, and John Todd all had counties named after them. Hugh McGary, who survived, did not. He received much of the blame for faults that others shared—rashness and reckless courage. The names of all the dead still are not known.

Daniel Boone, who lost his son Israel, went on to live another 38 years, dying in Missouri. He could not describe his son's death without tears. Since the boy was just recovering from fever, he had urged him to stay home. But Israel had insisted on sharing the danger with his father.

When Robert Patterson returned to Lexington, the town he founded, he gave Aaron Reynolds a horse and saddle and 200 acres of prime land as thanks for saving his life. Benjamin Netherland later went to Jessamine County and built a hotel called Mingo Tavern. He became the first postmaster of Nicholasville.

Because of the battle, 1782 is known as Kentucky's "year of blood." Contrary to popular belief, Blue Licks was not the last battle of the American Revolution. Later, for revenge, there was an expedition to Ohio where two Indian towns were burned. There were other battles and many other killings. The Battle of Blue Licks was, though, the worst defeat Kentuckians had ever suffered. It was a milestone in the ongoing battle against the British and Indians, a contest that was not decided until after the War of 1812.